Between Two Seasons of Happiness

Between Two Seasons of Happiness

IRENE DISCHE

ILLUSTRATED BY DANIEL PUDLES

BLOOMSBURY

First published in Great Britain in 1998
Bloomsbury Publishing Plc, 38 Soho Square, London W1V 5DF

The moral right of the author has been asserted
A CIP catalogue record of this book is available from the
British Library

ISBN 0 7475 4023 3 Paperback
ISBN 0 7475 4029 2 Hardback

Printed in Great Britain by Clays Ltd, St Ives plc

10 9 8 7 6 5 4 3 2 1

Cover design by Michelle Radford

For Emily and Leon, and also for Pali – I.D.
For Laure – D.P.

Right up to March 2, 1944, which is really not all that long ago, Dr Nagel, a stern old village doctor, liked to grumble that his hot-hearted son Laszlo was a stranger to him.

'Laszlo is all fiery feeling,' he murmured out of the window to the new morning, as his valet crouched at his side, struggling to knot the doctor's brown bow tie.

'Laszlo takes too many chances,' he told the heavy wooden door of his office, before entering to begin a day's work.

'Laszlo has not got the sense that the Nagel men have always had,' he muttered into his teacup, sitting in the library, as he did every afternoon.

'It has always been like that with your father, so you are lucky to be in my care,' he said to his grandson Peter. 'Laszlo Nagel has no talent for moderation.' Moved by his own words, Dr Nagel sighed and patted the boy on the head. The boy fought back his tears.

●　●　●

Once upon a time not so very long ago, when Dr Nagel's rakish son Laszlo was still a student in Budapest, he paid a visit to his hometown. His stay was short, but long enough for him to fall in love with a neighbour's freckle-faced red-haired niece Dalia, on a visit from Germany. She was sixteen and he was twenty and he told her he could go blind from looking at such a sweet combination of eyes, nose and mouth, could go deaf listening to her lilting voice, could go mad by feeling her soft hand. He shivered as he spoke. But he was warm, even his black hair always felt warm to the touch.

Dalia never had a chance to question her own heart; Laszlo overwhelmed her with his.

When he came to see Dalia again a few weeks later, she allowed him to steer her into the garden for a kiss, and then she began to cry. Tears splashing over her freckles, she told him his first visit had been fruitful enough: she was pregnant. He did not comfort her, but rushed to his room, and leaning out of his window, he set off firecrackers he had been saving for an occasion. The wedding was remembered by all the townspeople for its joyous, extravagant party. It seemed that half of Germany had crowded into the village. Even Dr Nagel had clearly enjoyed himself.

On the day of Dalia's seventeenth birthday, red-haired Peter was born. Dr Nagel had come to Budapest a few weeks earlier to deliver the baby himself. He was an excellent physician and did not trust his grandchildren to any other doctor's care. The baby pleased him. 'A quiet child,' said Dr Nagel with relief, 'more like his mother than his father.' He had doubled Laszlo's allowance, and now

he paid for a nanny and household help; Laszlo was finishing his legal studies. Dr Nagel had been disappointed that his only son had not wanted to become a doctor, but he only complained about this occasionally, and he was mollified when Laszlo stumbled into a well paying job in the diplomatic service. It was not just luck. Laszlo Nagel had charm and good manners, a friendly face and the energy of an optimist: he would do well in an organisation. Dr Nagel wanted to show his son that he approved of him, and gave him a spectacular present: a car.

The car was fast, shiny and black. Laszlo told Dalia to kiss the toddler goodbye; they were going to go for a drive. He drove very fast, and when his wife closed her eyes in fright, he took her hand and squeezed it. 'He's too passionate about things,' Dr Nagel always complained. Perhaps there was a nail or some glass on the road. One of the tyres burst. Laszlo could not hold the steering wheel with his left hand alone. The car slammed into a tree. His hold on Dalia's hand was not tight enough: she was killed. He escaped with bumps and scratches on his handsome exterior.

After Dalia died, Laszlo Nagel felt very sad but he could not change his nature; he enjoyed being alive. He soon had a reputation in Budapest as a merry widower.

He was also a merry father. He sometimes took a day off from work just to play with his son. 'Play' was his word; observers would have said something like 'gallivant', or 'carouse'. He took Peter for journeys to the parts of town where serious adults did not venture. Propping him on his shoulder, he pushed through a crowd to see a cockfight. He took him to see the central courthouse and after that, the biggest jail. He chatted with strangers on the street who had not shaved or washed in months, or people who looked like they were about to rob a bank. He liked to say, 'I'm a good-luck man'.

Laszlo's son accepted his explanations for

everything, including the story that he had purchased him in a speciality store for red-headed babies. When Peter asked his father to buy another sibling, he consented. He took him to the same strange, dusty little town where he had bought him just a few years earlier. Laszlo simply could not find the store, so they went to a carnival instead, which was just as good.

When the locusts came in such numbers one spring that people spoke of a plague, Laszlo spent the afternoons observing them; he could tell the males and the females apart. Peter watched him scavenging through the bushes of the small park on the corner, his fancy jacket dragging on the ground.

Peter knew that his father was not afraid of anything, not of dogs that barked and gnashed their teeth at them in a village, nor of the reproaches of his father, Dr Nagel, who came to stay the weekend once a month and would say, on the very first evening of each visit, 'Laszlo, this is impossible.'

On those evenings, Laszlo dismissed the nanny and put Peter to bed himself, although Dr Nagel disapproved of this. It was a job for the servants. Dr Nagel could not stop him, and while Laszlo helped Peter to brush his teeth, the old man waited impatiently to continue a conversation about Laszlo's shortcomings. Leaving the bathroom, Laszlo cocked his head to listen, and heard the old man's feet pacing downstairs in the living room. He frowned, lay down flat on the floor, and pressed his ear to the floorboards, gesturing for Peter to do the same. They lay there together, listening.

'Hear your grandfather?' asked Laszlo, 'How he is pacing? Worry, worry, worry. He is worried about us. Ah. Hear the glass? He's stopped to take a sip of brandy. Quite right. It's cold outside. And now? More pacing.'

Laszlo hopped up, swept his son into his arms, and said, 'What are you lying on the cold floor for!' He dropped the boy with a wild lack of ceremony onto the middle of the

15

bed, and Peter's giggles travelled through the house. The pacing downstairs stopped abruptly. 'Oh heavens, he's listening in on us,' said Laszlo. 'I am a doomed man! "Children should be kept calm before bedtime", he will say.'

He sat down on the edge of the bed, held his son's hand, studied his face and whispered, 'Oh well, at least I know you'll have your own mind when you grow up. You won't be afraid of anything. You won't even be afraid to die. But you will like living. Oh yes, you will enjoy living very much. And your hands are sticky. We forgot to wash your hands. Never mind that now.'

Dr Nagel's pacing began again downstairs. Laszlo stroked Peter's forehead, looked into his eyes and whispered on, about aesthetics, about architecture, about how some people behaved like pigs, although that was a mean thing to say about pigs. Peter, noting that his strange words did not alter the basic merriness of his father's face, fell asleep in the warmth of that affectionate gaze.

Several years into Laszlo Nagel's widow-hood, when Peter was already six, he was sent to spend a few weeks with his grand-father. The weeks stretched into months. He was old enough to miss his father horribly. Dr Nagel's home was like a foreign country to him, with strange but rigorous customs he had to learn. The meals served in the kitchen marked days that were spent with Martha, one of the maids. Martha had a long pimply face, very long legs, and a sway back; although she was just in her late teens, she looked like a tired old mare, and she fol-lowed Dr Nagel's orders precisely.

'No sweets for children, ever,' said Dr Nagel in a neutral tone of voice. Sweets were eaten by the devil. No allowing them into the hands of sweet children.

'No talking if there is no point to it,' said Dr Nagel, his low voice flowing evenly through his throat, and never varying in intensity. 'Naps from 12.30 to 2.30.'

Since Dr Nagel had not prohibited it, Martha shared her interest in the kings and queens of Europe and told the small boy stories about them. She glanced around to see if anyone was listening and confided in him; she was honoured to look after something as rare as a fair-haired freckle-faced child. 'I have pink freckles, don't I?' she laughed, and patted her own cheeks unhappily.

'Twice a day Peter may visit the cat,' said Dr Nagel. Twice a day, Martha quietly allowed him into the living room to see Archibald, the angry old calico cat who could be found, day or night, in the same corner of the sofa. Archibald did not like company. If anyone came too close, he hissed and ran away. Once a day Peter played football outside on the lawn with Igor the chauffeur. Igor did not have the build of an athlete, he had sloping shoulders that no uniform could bolster, a round belly and a duck walk, but he was a great shot. He could place the ball 'like a god', as he always bragged. He enjoyed

playing with the little boy. 'Strenuous physical activity once a day is enough for anyone,' said Dr Nagel.

Peter rarely ventured beyond the lawn on one side, or the garden on the other. Dr Nagel declared even the next-door house, where Peter's dead mother had spent several months before marrying Laszlo, off limits, because the neighbours had referred to the child as 'poor motherless thing'. The mere mention of the word 'mother' made Peter uneasy.

Once, when Peter was in the living room, he noticed a framed photograph of his father propped on the mantelpiece. It was just a small gold-framed image of a smiling man with black hair and black eyes, and part of one cheek was hidden by a spray of pink flowers in a vase standing on the mantelpiece next to the photograph. At once the rest of the room, the rest of the world, lost all of its importance, all colour, all detail. That face was all that mattered. But that face, jailed in a golden frame, could not come to him.

Peter was shocked by his sudden longing for his father. If he had known how to name his feeling he might have said 'love', if he had known how to describe the feeling he would have said 'loss'. He stood in front of the picture for a very long time, and then Martha found him there and gave him a banana to cheer him up. Her solicitude surprised him. He was too sad to consider that someone else might notice what he was feeling. As he ate the banana, he heard Martha speaking to Dr Nagel in the library, and then Igor appeared and took him outside to play football for the second time that day.

A week later, it began to rain. It was raining all over Hungary. When the rain did not let up, the word 'flooding' entered adult conversation. The river was going to flood. The staff in Dr Nagel's house talked in low frightened voices about the prospect of a really big flood. One evening, in a deafening downpour, the headlights of Laszlo Nagel's new black car poked through the gloom, and lit up the front door. Peter heard the car horn honking cheerfully. He climbed up on a windowsill to see his father walk through the rain. He carried a new, crimson ladies' umbrella.

Laszlo did not bother to close the umbrella, but left it dripping in the hallway. He waltzed about with Peter, who gasped with delight and wrapped himself tightly, as permanently as he could, around his father's neck. But he had to release his grasp when Laszlo put him down to embrace his own father. Peter watched Dr Nagel's face as his son's arms hugged him; the old man grimaced.

'I'm taking the little one for a drive,' said Laszlo Nagel. 'Even though it's night-time. Even though it's raining.' He sent Martha to get Peter dressed warmly, and with Dr Nagel protesting, he guided him through the rain under his crimson umbrella to the car. 'I have something interesting to show you.' When they were in the car, Laszlo remembered Archibald. He disappeared again. Peter saw the front door open and shut twice, and then his father was back, Archie protesting loudly from under his jacket. 'There are some things even a cat should see,' said Laszlo Nagel.

He had brought blankets, and Peter felt comfortable. With the rain going 'shhhhh', and the car rocking him, he soon fell asleep. Laszlo woke his son when he stopped the car, the headlights shining on a seething dark mass nearby. It was the River Danube. 'Look how fast it's flowing,' said Laszlo. 'And it's growing bigger and bigger. Any second now it'll rise over its banks.'

Archibald was curled up in the window, his eyes gleaming resentfully. 'You're not scared, are you?' he asked Peter.

'No.'

'No reason to be. You're with me and I'm a good-luck man.'

Peter felt happy, not scared, sitting next to his father, the wind shaking the car fitfully, in an agitated but helpless way. Peter studied his father in the darkness; leaning forwards at the steering wheel, his face turned patiently in the direction of the river. Sometimes Laszlo looked down and spoke to him. 'Lots of things are just like this river. Ladies have a way of changing their sizes and shapes and personalities. You'll see. So do some countries. Hungary was bigger once, not so long ago. Today, it's just a little country, about as big as a pond. 'Look, Peter.' Laszlo pointed to a group of bushes.

'Past the bushes, if you kept going, you'd reach Germany. Say "Germany".'

'Germany.'

'That's good. Germany used to be small. It consisted of several little streams that came together and made a river. Now it's large, and maybe it'll grow larger. Do you understand what I'm saying, Peter?'

'Yes.'

'Try to sleep instead. I'll wake you when the river rises.'

Some time in the night he began to drive again. The river had swollen even more and overflowed its banks. When Peter woke up in the morning, they were parked on a hill above a road. Down below, the street was underwater, and the trees seemed shorter, their lower branches dipping into the thick brown soup. His father was sitting on the hood of the car, under his red umbrella, staring at the landscape. Archibald was purring. He probably felt he had no choice. Peter knocked on the window.

'When we return home, your grandfather will just be sitting down to breakfast all dressed up for the day,' said Laszlo, climbing back inside. 'He'll be wearing his brown suit, and his brown bow tie. But he will object to brown mud all over this car.'

The ride back home was bumpy, and led through thick banks of mud that slopped on to the car, to the amusement of the driver and concern of his two passengers.

Dr Nagel was sitting down to breakfast in

his neat brown suit and bow tie. The maid was bending over to serve him coffee. The radio was standing in the middle of the table. Dr Nagel had sat there all night listening to news of the flood, and waiting for his family to return, and he was extremely angry. 'You're a stranger to me,' he said to Laszlo. 'And that poor cat.'

Martha came to take charge of Peter, but Laszlo told his son to sit down and have some breakfast, while he sat down next to his frowning father. 'I'm leaving Hungary,' he said.

Laszlo Nagel had been offered a diplomatic posting to Berlin, in Germany.

It was 1938, which is really not all that long ago, but a lot of things were different. His father protested. The Germans had their heads full of strange ideas. It would be dangerous there. His son Laszlo responded, 'Nonsense. I'm a good-luck man.'

Of course he took Peter with him.

• • •

In the late summer of 1938, Laszlo Nagel

came to pick Peter up from Dr Nagel's house. The boy scrambled into the hot back seat of the car, and then turned around to wave to his grandfather. Dr Nagel glanced at his grandson and twiddled his fingers in the air. But he forgot to stand up very straight and allowed his jacket to hang open, so that Peter saw his crisp white shirt, his braces, and the way his thin neck seemed overburdened by his big old head. Leaving his grandfather behind suddenly struck Peter as an unkindness. 'Why don't you come along?' he shrieked through the car window. His grandfather looked cross, put his fingers to his lips and said, 'Be quiet, child.'

As Laszlo started the car, Martha came cantering from the house, steaming with determination, and he had to turn the engine off again and accept the large, red cloth bag that she handed him.

Just as he started the car again, the maid came out with Archibald squirming and furious in her arms, and then the gardener

27

came, and the cook, drying her hands on her apron, and finally Igor, waving a football. Martha was the first to wipe tears from her eyes and the cook followed suit, while the gardener blinked, the maid clutched Archibald to her chest, Igor pretended to kick the ball, and Dr Nagel pursed his lips. A peasant bicycling along the road with a basket stopped short, in order to see what was going on. Her skirts flapped loudly in the breeze.

Laszlo and Peter left anyway, driving in silence away from the house, driving in silence through the town. Summer seemed to have exploded; the air was full of blossom that rained in through the open windows. When they reached the outskirts, Laszlo pulled over at the side of the road and sighed with relief. He opened Martha's bag, looked inside, and tossed it to Peter. It proved to be stuffed with sweets and chocolates.

'We have a very long drive to our new house,' said Laszlo.

• • •

Their new house in Berlin was not a house at all, but an apartment in a large building on a broad avenue in the centre of the city. Laszlo had shipped all their furniture from Budapest, so the dark, high-ceilinged rooms were instantly recognisable as home.

'This city is ours,' whispered Laszlo, 'but the others don't know it. Don't give us away. Pretend we are just borrowing it.'

The city air was cool, the sky pale, the streets full of cars, and everything was strange – how could it belong to him? The people looked strange, and they dressed strangely. The courtyard smelled of shrubbery, not of cabbage, as courtyards did in Budapest. It was vast, and one did not overhear everyone's conversations, as one did in Budapest. And finally, he could not understand what anyone was saying anyway. No one spoke Hungarian. At the nearby school he attended (his father escorting him there, Peter savouring each of those last precious minutes with him), Peter watched the

children babbling and felt terror and amaze-
ment that they could make sense of the peculiar syllables they produced. He followed
the hands that pulled at his elbows to get him
to the right classroom, sat numbly, dumbly
through lessons, and followed the corridors
to the entrance hall at noon, pushed through
the huge wooden door, and watched his own
feet tread the pavement till they reached the
first tree at the curb where he finally looked
up at the slender feminine figure invariably
standing there. A hand tousled his head. And
then this figure escorted him home. That was
Thea, the housekeeper, and she too, could
only utter these strange senseless sounds.
Thea had two thin blonde plaits that were
wrapped tightly around her head, and a wide
white face with hooded blue eyes that he pre-
ferred not to look at. He knew her by her
pleasant, salty smell and her way of holding
his hand, the fingers laced, so that he could
not let go. After a few weeks, certain syllables
that occurred frequently became familiar, and

after another few weeks they assumed meaning. And soon he passed without any effort on his part into the realm of those who could speak German.

Gradually the house became familiar. His father was his guide. When footsteps stomped downward on the stairs, Laszlo would sit back to listen, put his finger in the air and say 'Aha. Dr Schneider from upstairs is going out. Dr Schneider must be treated with caution. Because Dr Schneider is a Professor.' And he allowed Peter to open the door a crack and look at the descending closely-cropped blonde head. 'Be polite!' his father said. He liked to take Peter into his study and chat. When he switched on a huge radio with many dials, Peter knew he had to pay close attention to what he was saying. Laszlo spoke softly, despite the blaring of the radio. 'Be watchful. Keep your eyes open. But never let anyone know that you have a mind that works. They don't like it.'

Peter began to watch everyone. He especially liked to watch Frau Bilka who lived on the ground floor from where she tended something she called 'order'. 'Hier heerscht Ordnung,' she always crowed: Order Rules. Her teeth were disorderly, brown and crowded in her mouth, except for a gap between the two front teeth, so that when she said, 'Order' or 'Good morning' or 'Good day' or 'Good evening', one could see her tongue writhing in her mouth.

And the neighbourhood became familiar too. At first the street downstairs had seemed to him a big loud windy space with cars hurtling back and forth and a pavement with strangers pushing past, and all this activity seemed utterly random although conducted with an air of purpose. Soon, the street downstairs consisted of many little parts, each with its own significance. A store right in the house sold specialities of the Rhineland. The shop window was set up like a stage in a theatre, with curtains draped on either side of a group of wine bottles and sausages in apparent conversation. Herr Bauer was a small round man with a Rhine accent and the cheerfulness, said Peter's father, that all Rhinelanders have. His fingers were round and red, like some of the sausages he sold.

Herr Bauer was a great friend of Frau Bilka's, because they had an enemy in common: the pigeons. The pigeons liked to build nests in any nook or cranny and the best nooks that the house had to offer were on a ledge along the first floor, just over Frau Bilka's favourite window, the one she liked to rest her elbows on to watch the street, and over Herr Bauer's shop front. The pigeons roosted there, and their droppings and feathers rained down on Herr Bauer's shop window and on Frau Bilka's grey head. So the two allies were staging a big offensive against the birds, using all their cunning to drive them from the house.

Frau Bilka had made the first move. Her young nephew spent one Sunday laying

broken glass along the ledge. But the birds felt no discomfort sitting on it. 'Now it's your turn to do something, Mr Neighbour,' said Frau Bilka. 'I don't want to get the police involved yet.'

So Herr Bauer inflated a huge quantity of balloons and taped them along the ledge. 'The house looks like a circus, Mr Neighbour, that will never do,' said Frau Bilka. 'Although I must admit it works.'

So Herr Bauer took the balloons down again and it was Frau Bilka's turn to think of something. Frau Bilka's nephew returned and laid poison along the ledge. But the birds seemed to thrive on it. Herr Bauer's turn.

Every morning before Herr Bauer opened for business, he set up his ladder in front of the shop window, and you could hear his knees squeaking as he climbed up the rungs with his broom, and, teetering dangerously on the top rung, swept the ledge clean over his shop. Then he came down, closed the ladder and dragged it over to Frau Bilka's window. He opened it, climbed up again, teetered once more, and swept the ledge clean again. The pigeons took at least a day to return. And that was the end of the matter until Frau Bilka came up with a better idea. But she wouldn't. The arrangement suited her perfectly. 'Just don't die on me, Herr Bauer,' she liked to say. 'Those pigeons will eat me alive.'

'Don't laugh at the neighbours,' warned Laszlo, the radio blaring in the background. 'Hide what you think as if your thoughts are the Queen's jewels.'

Peter did not laugh at Frau Bilka; he ripped his mouth into a wide smile whenever he passed her. He imitated his father, who always smiled broadly when he didn't want to be bothered by someone. Smiling was simple and indisputable. He felt cheerful. As Peter got to know the city, he liked it more and more. He could identify the uniforms people wore—not only policemen, postmen and the different kinds of soldiers, but also the children. He admired the pretty red flags that hung everywhere, with an amusing symbol in the middle called a swastika. His father often wore a swastika on his jacket too. Peter liked swastikas so much that he drew them all over the Hungarian picture books he had from home, so that in the end he could not look at the pictures anymore. He found it nearly impossible to get the direction of the swastika hooks right.

A few weeks passed, and he knew the different cracks in the pavement, and how their street connected to other streets, and how they connected to the city zoo, to the train station. And when his father said, 'Now this city really belongs to us, you see?', he felt proud of their secret.

The time without his father had frightened him, and he only felt really happy when his father was there, within touching distance. He accepted that this could not always be the case. He made the best of the substitute, Thea Schmidt. She was a warm-hearted, bad-tempered woman. Once, when Peter spilled a glass of milk, her hand descended from up high and walloped his cheek. She did not apologise afterwards, or comfort him. She bristled with indignation and snapped, 'That will teach you.' Within days this form of education, which she named *ohrfeigen* had become standard. Peter soon grew accustomed to the sting, to the ringing in his ears afterwards, and the red stain it left on his cheek.

Thea Schmidt did not mean to be cruel. She simply had a shortage of something called patience, which is really a wonderful form of helplessness. She did not like to be helpless. At least her moods were predictable. If he misbehaved, she let him have it. She protected him, too. If something worried him, he told her and she took care of it. When a boy in school taunted him about his red hair, she waited at the school entrance the next morning, and when he appeared, Thea Schmidt bent down to him and hissed, 'Peter is new here. You look after him, or I'll look after you.'

The boy became Peter's friend, in as much as Peter had any friends. He felt very shy of children his own age. He cared too much about his father to waste energy caring about anyone else. Only Thea forced herself on his attention. He soon came to admire her.

When Dr Schneider, the upstairs Professor, passed them on the staircase in the morning, and remarked to Thea that she, 'a good German girl', shouldn't work for foreigners, she fell silent, and didn't speak for the rest of the way to school. When Peter asked her what the matter was, she squeezed his hand and shook her head. Her blue eyes looked opaque. Peter noted that Dr Schneider (a tall handsome blonde man with a flat head), had similar blue eyes. The next morning, Thea took a watering can along to school. 'The hedge downstairs is drying up,' she explained. She made Peter wait at a distance while she sprinkled the hedge. When she heard Dr Schneider's footsteps come down the stairs, she hesitated. As he passed her on the narrow walk in front of the house (Frau Bilka watching from the window), she turned, bumping into him. As she stumbled, the contents of the watering can tipped all over his suit.

'I'm so sorry!' she cried. The professor was drenched. She put down the can, carelessly, and stretched her hard hand out to Peter, winking at him. 'We're late; we have to hurry.'

Thea was reliable; she never forgot a thing; she never went away, and if her hand on his cheek was hard, the rest of her was soft and pretty and punctual. And when Laszlo Nagel came home, she became nicer: she was not impatient or bad-tempered then. In the early evening, she disappeared discreetly, and never interfered with his way of doing things.

Laszlo Nagel hated regularity of any kind. Dinner took place whenever they chose to have it. They often went downstairs to Herr Bauer and bought sausage from him, and then they boarded a tram and rode along, eating. When the last bite had been swallowed, they rang the bell to get off the tram. 'The sausage decides our route,' said Laszlo, who never went anywhere without a map, a knife, a bottle opener, and a few pieces of liquorice. He loved liquorice. 'The world is divided into those who love chocolate and those who love liquorice,' he said. 'Have you noticed?'

He adored taking Peter to the cinema, or to the circus. 'It is necessary for strong men,' he said, 'to spend at least one night a week in the cinema, and at least one afternoon a month in the circus.'

Sometimes he said, 'Let's get dressed up and go somewhere unbearably fancy for dinner.' Then he spent quite a while in front of the mirror, because he was careful about the way he looked, combing his thick black hair and straightening a tie he had put on for the occasion. He had bought Peter a suit too, and a new, dark blue, Loden winter coat with buttons made of horn, just like his own. Except for the difference in their hair colour, thought Peter, they looked like a pair.

Sometimes it turned out they were invited to someone's house. Laszlo would introduce his son formally: 'I've brought Peter Nagel along,' or 'May I introduce Peter Nagel?'. And Peter would sit at his right hand. He followed his father's example and talked about the weather or sporting events. He tried to stay on the alert for amusing details – Herr Herrman's tie had lain for a whole minute in his soup, and then he had taken it out surreptitiously and the soup had dribbled in a stream down into his trousers – that he could share later with his father. After a while these parties became boring; a string quartet would play, or the talk just went on and on, lulling him to sleep. But time seemed to sympathise with Peter, time shortened itself for his benefit. In one minute he was sitting in a crowded room, in the next his father was carrying him through the night, and laying him down in the car.

One evening Laszlo decided to take Peter to a nightclub.

The club was full of beautifully dressed women and men in uniform dancing or sitting in groups around shiny black tables. Each table had a telephone, and strangers could call each other up and chat.

They chose a table, sat down, and Laszlo told Peter to order. 'I have an accent in German, and you don't,' he said. 'They don't like accents in this place.' When the waiter came, Laszlo pretended to be a deaf mute, and Peter ordered juice for them both, instead of wine, while his father pinched him furiously under the table.

Soon the telephone rang. Two women addressed them from the next table. 'You two are not in uniform,' they sang into the receiver. 'What are you doing here?'

'Waiting to dance with you,' Laszlo

45

replied, no longer worried about his accent.

The two women rose from their seats revealing fluffy dark dresses. They looked like vultures as they swooped slowly towards them. They were mother and daughter. And they smelled like they had come directly from an arbour of roses. 'Well, then let's dance!' they agreed.

The younger one already had Laszlo's hand in her grasp, and her mother stretched a hand with red fingernails towards Peter. His father was moving towards the dance floor, so he had no choice. He allowed the talon to close on his hand, and lead him away. She danced carefully with him, she showed him the steps, and after a while she heaved him up in the air, pressed him against her bosom, and danced with him high up in her arms.

'Little man,' she said. 'Where is your mother?'

'I don't have one,' he said, struggling out of her grasp again, daring the long drop to the floor again.

balut undergarment

She held him by the tips of the fingers, and shuffled her feet. 'Is that what you are doing in Berlin? Looking for a mother perhaps?'

'Oh no!' he said, moving his feet too. 'No! We live here now.'

'Do you have a lot of money?' she asked.

'Yes,' he said.

'That's nice,' she replied. 'I would love to see it. I'm tired now. My name is Frau Weltecke. What's yours?'

They all sat down at the table again and this time Laszlo's partner, Fräulein Weltecke, ordered a bottle of wine. She was even more inquisitive than her mother.

'What is your job?' Fräulein Weltecke asked Laszlo.

'I'm an expert,' he replied, 'An Engineer. I build underground tunnels and canals for Germany. You don't want to hear the details, it's very boring. I work hard. My son does too. He goes to school. We rarely have a chance for amusement. So this is a great pleasure.

Meeting two such beautiful women.'

Peter held back the protest forming on his lips about his father's fibs. He did not know why, but he felt afraid. When Frau Weltecke turned to him and said, 'Do you have a car?' he replied, 'Oh no.'

'You don't have a car ...' she repeated despondently. 'Oh well. No car and no mother. And probably no bank account.'

Laszlo overheard and interrupted. 'Of course we have a bank account, although Hungarians like us are not permitted to have them these days, and we will soon have to find a German to whom we can just give the money. I believe that's the done thing these days for foreigners, giving one's money away. And then the new owner gives a little back, every so often, if one really, really needs it. Am I right? We also have a car. Shall I drive you ladies home? Because we have to go now.' Mother and daughter looked at each other and nodded. So they all left together.

'What a car!' they exclaimed, although it

was quite an ordinary car.

Frau Weltecke sat down in the front seat next to Laszlo, and Fräulein Weltecke sat behind next to Peter. Laszlo drove very fast through the back streets until he reached a wide, nearly deserted avenue that led through a park. He accelerated. Frau Weltecke lay back in the seat, closed her eyes and whimpered, while in the back seat, Fräulein Weltecke grabbed hold of Peter's hand and held it over her own eyes.

Everyone was flung forwards as Laszlo Nagel applied the brakes, screeching to a halt in front of the address the two women had given him. They each gave an identical loud groan of relief, wiggled out of the car, and slammed the doors huffily behind them.

Laszlo put his feet down on the accelerator again, speeding from the curb, and gunned the motor so that Peter was thrown backwards again in the seat. The boy cowered.

'Don't tell me you're afraid to die?'

marvelled his father.

He slowed down. 'I'm sorry if I frightened you,' he said sincerely. 'I showed off for the ladies. I wanted to make the evening worth their while. It was interesting to me that two ordinary fellows like us could amuse ourselves in a night club for high-ranking Nazis.'

Peter knew what Nazis were. They were the bosses in Germany, they made the rules. People often spoke about them, pronouncing the word 'Nazi' exuberantly, with pride. He had seen many pictures of the boss of all the Nazis called the Führer, who was pudgy and dark-haired, and reminded him pleasantly of Igor his grandfather's chauffeur, except that Igor was a calm, friendly fellow, whereas the Führer was irritable. Peter often heard him scolding on the radio. But people loved him so much that thousands would assemble just to hear him speak. And when he began to scold really loudly, they cheered.

Since the Führer was obviously a dear, if cranky man, Peter was puzzled when his father remarked, 'The Nazis will not bother small fry like us.' But Peter's bewilderment gave way to wholehearted agreement when his father added, 'And besides, we're having a good time together, the two of us, aren't we?'

Laszlo rarely went out in the evening without Peter, and when he did, then it was an ironclad rule that Peter was allowed to wake his father up in the morning, no matter how late he had got in the night before. And then Laszlo would tell him about his evening, about the party he had attended, the people he had met, the meals he had eaten. 'I had pigeon last night, Herr Bauer and Frau Bilka would congratulate me. Roasted pigeon. And the head of the bank gave me tips on what to do with all my millions.'

Sometimes his father brought one or another of his evening companions home so that Peter could meet them too. He would find them in his father's bed in the morning, sometimes men sometimes women, but they were all friendly, and they never stayed long enough to stake any claim on Laszlo Nagel. Thea, in any case, wouldn't have tolerated it. She treated these visitors badly, with her most pungent impoliteness, to make sure they never returned.

● ● ●

Autumn came. It was colder in Berlin than it had been in Budapest. Peter was learning to read and write, and his father took an interest in his progress, and showed him how to read in Hungarian as well. 'I don't want you to forget Hungarian,' he said.

The first week of November, all the lakes froze over. 'The sky,' protested Thea, 'is luring people outside with bright blue colours, just to be cruel.' She cooked hot soup for them every day, and insisted they eat it for supper. Peter's father liked to stay home in the evenings now, anyway, and listen to the radio.

One Wednesday afternoon, Thea took Peter to the cinema after school. He knew there must be an explanation for this mid-week treat but she did not offer one. She was very cheerful. 'It's my birthday,' she finally admitted. 'Today is the 9th of November. It's a very special day.'

He had not thought of her as someone who might have a birthday.

The film was a comedy, the hall packed with a merry audience. Everyone enjoyed the same opinion about what was funny, and they laughed in unison, their laughter rolling like thunder. When the film finished, Peter was surprised to see that night had fallen. Thea stopped in at Herr Bauer's on the way home to buy chocolates filled with sweet liqueur: 'A present for myself.' Herr Bauer sighed several times and pressed his fat red fingers against his forehead. 'I am a little nervous today,' he said, 'because of the situation.' Peter did not know what a 'situation' was, and he noted to himself that it was something unpleasant. He tried to cheer Herr Bauer up.

'It's Thea's birthday!' he said.

His strategy worked. Herr Bauer beamed and pressed a bottle of champagne into Thea's hand. 'I've been looking for an excuse to give you a present,' he said.

She was preparing supper when Peter heard sounds of festivity out on the street. He ran to the kitchen to tell Thea the flattering news, that the whole city was celebrating her birthday. She was cooking at the stove, and he tugged at her skirt. 'Listen to that!' he said. 'Just for you!'

She turned around and said 'Nonsense!' in such a cross tone of voice that Peter ducked, expecting an *Ohrfeige*.

His father came home late, very late, with a spectacular bouquet of flowers and a box of chocolates for Thea. He handed them to her with the big smile that flashed all his white teeth and spelled absent-mindedness, and said, 'Happy Birthday, dear Thea. And now you must excuse me.' He rushed to his room and turned on the radio. He was concentrating so hard that he did not notice or object when Peter listened in. An important official had been murdered in Paris by a Jew. All the Jews of the world were going to be held responsible. They would be punished.

'Papa, have I ever seen a Jew?' asked Peter, sliding into the room. He did not think he had. He had often regretted it. In school, the children liked to laugh about Jews. Once, the teacher had drawn pictures of them on the blackboard, they had round heads and noses like corkscrews. She had taught the class a little poem about never trusting a Jew. Peter would have liked very much to see one of those strange-nosed fat men who were trying to run the whole world. He would stick his tongue out at them.

His father switched off the radio and his face took on an expression of pleasure and friendliness. 'Seen a Jew? Well, I don't know, maybe,' he said. 'Who knows. Let's have some dinner. We have a birthday to celebrate.'

Much later, when people were sleeping soundly, the night grew noisier and woke Peter. He crept out of bed. The clocks ticked. He went to the balcony, opened the door. Icy air enveloped him. He heard the sound of running and shouting. The sky was lit up in one corner. He wondered whether others were celebrating Thea's birthday too, and felt pleased that it was such an event. Then he heard the door to Thea's room open. She came out on the balcony, bringing warmth and her pleasant smell, her blonde hair loose on her shoulders. She stared at the sky. But she was not pleased with what she saw, and she took his hand, lacing his fingers in hers. 'It's completely ridiculous,' she grumbled. 'You're coming inside and going to bed.' She closed her door quietly.

Just as he was falling asleep again, something crashed downstairs. Peter pulled his blanket from his bed, wrapped it around his shoulders, and sneaked into the living room. He took a seat in an armchair. Footsteps

trampled up and down the stairs. Dr Schneider was having guests. He heard pounding upstairs now, stifled shouts, and something that might have been gasping. But the night did not want Peter to eavesdrop, the night sent its guard, sleep, to overwhelm him, right where he was nestled in the chair.

He woke up the next morning, still sitting upright in the chair, when his father hugged him. He did not think it odd to find Peter asleep in the living room. 'They had quite a party last night,' he said. 'No school today.'

Laszlo Nagel saw no reason to go to work, either. The party was still going on. The street was crowded with merrymakers. Thea cooked eggs and complained that they tasted smoky because the air now smelled of smoke. 'Don't go out on that balcony again,' she ordered, treating Laszlo, her employer, like a child too.

Laszlo took Peter out on the balcony. Peering over the railing, they could see that the pavement just outside their front door was covered with broken glass.

'You two are not to go outside today,' Thea said, her bossiness undiminished. Peter's father was already putting on his coat. Peter put his on too, and they ran downstairs. Herr Bauer's shop window had fallen into the street. The shards lay scattered in front of his shop, with a heap of broken wine bottles on top. The pigeons seemed to revel in the destruction, padding in circles among the broken glass, dipping their heads strangely, extending their feathers, weaving, dancing. They had pecked at the contents of the bottles. They were drunk.

Frau Bilka waved her big hands at them, but they were unimpressed. 'Such a mess!' she snapped at two soldiers who arrived with brooms. 'Order rules in this house!' They obviously had orders to clean up. As they swept up the glass, Frau Bilka marched up to them and said, 'Where is Herr Bauer, if I may ask?' 'Calm down, lady,' the soldiers muttered and kept sweeping.

'Then at least sweep the pigeons out of here,' she said, enraged, 'if Herr Bauer is not around to do it.'

She saw Laszlo, turned to him and snapped, 'I know exactly where Herr Bauer is. They threw him into the canal. He doesn't know how to swim.'

• • •

Peter and his father took a tram through the city. 'Her Bauer,' said Peter, 'will be all wet.'

His father made no reply. All over town, shop windows had been smashed. Policemen lounged in front of shops to prevent shoppers from entering. At one building, right off the city's biggest street, a fire was raging. Firemen stood watching, their hoses hanging limply in their hands, as if they had run out of water. But they did not look perturbed. An admiring crowd gathered to watch. 'Isn't it beautiful?' called a little girl. A man was led out of the next door building by several soldiers. Suddenly, he tripped. The soldiers surrounded him. Peter could see them jerking their legs inwards, as if they might be kicking something. The little girl's mother lifted her up so that she could have a better look. But the man was on his feet again, and the little group disappeared.

A whole class of school children arrived, milling about in the company of their teacher, who explained the damage as if they were touring an exhibition. The Jews, Peter heard the teacher say, had been taught a lesson.

Peter felt briefly a kind of exhilaration that the bad people had at last received their due. 'Serves them right, doesn't it, Daddy?' he asked.

But still his father made no reply. After a while, Laszlo tugged on his collar, and they left, walking along the wide avenue till they reached a coffee house.

'Order for both of us, Peter,' whispered his father. 'I would like some hot rum.'

Peter ordered apple cake and hot chocolate for them both. His father spoke softly, in Hungarian. 'The word Jew in Hungarian is *zsido*, Peter; it is an ugly word; it makes my skin crawl, just like the German word *Jude*. Why? Because it has been used as a taunt as long as I can remember.' Laszlo finished his hot chocolate on one gulp. 'But who is The Jew? Is he the little monster that your teacher drew on the blackboard? Or is he perhaps Herr Bauer? Perhaps it is Herr Bauer. Order me a rum, Peter. Cocoa is for children. Call the waiter, Peter.'

Peter did not.

So his father went on. 'Alternatively, there is no such thing as The Jew. There is such a thing as a Jewish person. In Hungarian: *Zsidoember*. A handsome sounding word. Applicable to, for instance, Herr Bauer. Because he practises the Jewish religion. Well, in fact, he doesn't, but his grandparents did. You are confused? I am poor at explaining. Now for God's sake order me a hot rum, Peter.' He banged his fist on the table, and everyone turned around and stared.

The boy called the waiter and ordered

another hot chocolate. His father sighed.

'Haven't you ever noticed the strange star painted on his shop window? That's a Jewish star. The Nazis painted it to show shoppers that Herr Bauer is a Jew, for we would otherwise not know it. Because of course Herr Bauer is first and foremost a Rhinelander.'

'I want to go home,' Peter said.

As they came in the door, they knew by the way Thea knocked the pots and pans in the kitchen, her feet pounding, that she was furious. 'We're staying in now!' Peter's father called in a cheerful voice, as if nothing were the matter. 'I'm not finished yet,' he said, and steered Peter into his study. He closed the door, and made Peter pull up a chair and sit down next to him at his desk. They sat shoulder to shoulder in silence until Laszlo finally spoke up. 'Our family is sort of Jewish, too. But we come from Hungary, so the Germans do not mind us at all. Laszlo reassured him. And then he said something that shocked Peter. 'Your mother was Jewish, from here.'

Peter's father had never used the word 'mother' before, and hearing that word come out of his mouth made Peter feel dizzy with surprise. Laszlo Nagel added, 'I must go and see whether her parents are all right. They have never wanted to see me. They were angry. They are very old. You'd better stay at home, or Thea will murder me.'

• • •

Two days later, Laszlo Nagel said 'I'm a good-luck man. But you haven't proved yourself in this respect.' He said this regretfully, and then he had tears in his eyes. They gathered force and spurted over his cheeks, something that often happened to him during a bout of heavy laughing. Peter thought perhaps his words were some sort of difficult joke.

But a big suitcase was standing in the hall, and Thea, standing next to it, had her coat on. She held up Peter's loden winter coat. 'Let's go,' she said.

Peter tried to put a stop to this chain of events. He was already six years old, but he had a childish tantrum when the doorbell rang and a taxi driver appeared. The driver had left the car in front of the door with the engine running in order to hurry things. Peter hurled himself around the hall beneath his father's gaze. When he careened into the hall mirror, the glass shattered and fell everywhere. His father did not move. While Thea rushed to sweep the glass up, he looked at Peter and said, 'Now it looks like the street did the other day, up here.'

His words and his calmness set Peter into motion again, hurtling around the foyer until a vase went flying through the air. 'That's good luck,' his father said brightly. 'A broken vase brings seven years of good luck.'

Laszlo picked his son up, kissed him tenderly on each cheek, and said, 'You've learned to read and write. I always knew it would be good for something. I will write to you once a week. You write back. Once a week. That way, we'll stay together.'

• • •

And so Peter Nagel left his father and returned to Hungary just a few months after leaving it, returning to the small town just a few miles from the northern border, returning to his grandfather's house, and to his regime. As before, his grandfather's house was a fiefdom of visitors and servants, bound by respect for the owner and ruled by the clock. House ritual ensured that life went smoothly on, that no calamity could upset the order of things: breakfast at seven, a ceremonial luncheon at one o'clock, high tea in the library at five, a light supper at eight o'clock. At ten, any lights still burning in the house, except for Dr Nagel's, were extinguished.

There had been several changes in the Nagel residence while Peter was away. Martha, the maid who had looked after him, had fallen in love with Igor the chauffeur. The couple had married thoughtlessly, as Dr Nagel like to complain, quitting his services abruptly to move to the city. A new chauffeur or maid was not deemed necessary. Dr Nagel quite liked to drive his car himself, and there were enough staff left in the house to look after Peter. The cook and the two remaining maids and the butler and the gardener had not fallen in love, being married already. One other member of the family had run away, possibly for love as well. Archibald, the cat, had disappeared one evening. He was seen at the other end of town courting a black newcomer the baker had imported from a farm; she was supposed to be an expert in chasing mice, but all she had done was catch Archibald.

Another reason Dr Nagel no longer needed a chauffeur, was because he no longer made house calls, since he had officially retired from his practice that autumn. But he continued to treat patients, receiving them every morning in his practice on the ground floor. He was a stern doctor who rarely dispensed tablets. His principal medication was a gruff assurance that nothing serious was the matter. Nothing that time wouldn't heal.

Despite all the extra time he now had, Dr Nagel's routine kept him busy. And Peter had now become a part of that routine, an item requiring organisation. The fact that Peter was now six, nearly seven years old, meant that Dr Nagel had to do an extra bit of organising, for the boy needed to learn something. So his grandfather hired a private teacher for him. She would teach him both Hungarian and German, because presumably Peter would soon return to his father's care in Berlin.

Fräulein Strecker came from Monday to Friday, like the week, a wizened old woman with five brown curls bouncing on her forehead, and five outfits. That is, she always wore the same brown suit, but each day she wore a different coloured scarf: on Mondays a white one, on Tuesdays a yellow one, on Wednesdays a red one, on Thursday a blue one and on Fridays, to celebrate the death of Christ, a black one. She ruled over Peter fiercely, rapping him across the knuckles when he didn't pay attention, and forcing him to take a nap for two hours after lunch. She posted herself in a chair outside the door of the nursery, studying a succession of big books she referred to as 'antiquity', while making sure he stayed quiet.

Peter's simple but cosy room on the top floor of the house had a bed, a dressing table, a desk and a window. The window was positioned high up in the wall and showed only the sky. He could lie on his bed and look at the window as if it were an empty screen. He soon realised that he harboured in his memory all the films he had seen in Berlin, and that he could project them with his imagination onto the screen. Sometimes parts were missing but if he concentrated he could restore them. He played the films again and again. Unbeknownst to Fräulein Strecker, he spent every afternoon at the cinema.

When she let him out, it was time for tea. He always escorted her to the front door and waited for the door to close behind her. He would then wait for a while longer to make sure she was gone, peaking through the window at her narrow back as it marched into the darkness, while the clock turned him over to the care of his grandfather.

These sessions with his grandfather began silently with breakfast in the morning, and resumed in near silence at tea in the library. His grandfather seldom spoke. He was neither agreeable nor disagreeable. He sat at the breakfast table and ate, just as he sat in the library in a high-backed wooden chair and drank his tea. This was done with the minimum of movement or emotion. Sometimes he cleared his throat. Sometimes he asked Peter a question: 'How are you?'

And Peter would reply, 'Fine, thank you.'

'Would you like another glass of tea?'

'Yes, please.'

'Ahem,' he would clear his throat to the butler. 'We need more tea for Peter, please.'

'Please note, Peter, that only one sugar lump fits in each glass.'

After tea, Peter would go to the living room to see his father, in the gold-framed photograph, and then he went to his room until the supper bell rang. Supper was conducted in silence. After supper he went to his room until his grandfather appeared with one of the maids, and said from the doorway, 'It is bedtime.' The maid helped him to get ready for bed and gave him a peck on the cheek when his head was on the pillow, and he quickly fell asleep. So the week went.

On every Saturday, without fail, a letter from Peter's father arrived. Peter always spent Saturday morning perched on the high stone wall surrounding the house. From there he could see the postman as he approached their street corner. As soon as he had spotted the grey uniform, he sprang down from the wall and raced towards him. His grandfather didn't allow the postman to hand out the post to his grandson. 'I've got something for you,' the postman would say. 'You'll have to wait.' The boy would accompany him to the house and watch while the postman handed his letter over to the butler, who brought it to his grandfather's study. At high tea that afternoon, the letter would be lying on the library table, and Dr Nagel would give Peter permission to pick it up and open it.

Laszlo Nagel's handwriting began neatly at the top of the page – Peter never had any trouble deciphering the 'Dearest Most Beloved Son' – thereafter his writing settled into a slant, as if words were pouring downwards, until his letter became an illegible splash of ink.

There was nothing for Peter to do but ask his grandfather for help. Every week, he asked him, 'Please, grandfather, read it to me', and every week the old man made a disapproving face but took the letter, unfolded it carefully, as if this was a difficult task, and read it aloud to him.

'One can always read one's son's handwriting,' he would remark, 'no matter how much of a stranger he is.'

The letters were long cheerful descriptions of their house (what Frau Bilka was doing, what Thea was saying), of the city, of the parties, and of the ladies and gentlemen of Berlin society. The letters always promised a reunion as soon as the situation allowed it, and predicted in fact that the situation would improve, because, after all, 'I'm a good-luck man and don't you forget it.' Peter's father unfailingly closed with happy outbursts of affection for the reader he called, 'my one and only favourite son.'

'That last bit you'd better read to yourself, it's none of my business at all,' his grandfather would say. 'If you can't read it, there's nothing lost either.'

All week long, Peter worked on his replies, trying to make them equally witty and just as cheerful, even if he didn't feel the slightest bit cheerful or witty. Peter wrote to his father about town life, although he saw little of it and therefore had to make things up; he wrote about the guests his grandfather had, although his grandfather had hardly any, so Peter had to make them up too, and about Fräulein Strecker, whom he didn't have to make up at all, because she existed like the week.

Peter never dared tell his father that Dr Nagel read his letters out loud to him. He wrote, 'Your handwriting is hard to read, but of course I can manage it.' Only the last lines of Peter's letters were wholly true, because they stated a simple fact: 'How I miss you, Papa.'

And his father wrote back exuberant, witty letters. Sometimes he wrote about unpleasant incidents, but he always made them sound funny. Often he just wrote about the weather. 'All week,' he wrote, 'the weather has been trying to drive me out of Germany. I stayed in as much as possible. Finally today I ventured out. The sky was just waiting. It tipped grey and white slop on me, thundering uproariously as I scurried back inside. Now it's gathering strength ...'

And invariably he closed with those tender outpourings that his grandfather refused to read aloud, because they were so foreign to him, so immoderate.

'And this part, you can make out yourself, it is between you and your father,' Dr Nagel would sniff. 'A thousand hugs and kisses – that would take a long time to administer. You'd miss dinner.'

Dr Nagel never ever said any overly nice word to anyone; Peter could not imagine he ever had. He was not drawn to his grandfather. He was put off by the skin that was rough as bark on his face and hands, the lichen-like moustache, his smell of toilet water, disinfectant and tobacco. But he respected him, as everyone did. Dr Nagel knew better. Dr Nagel knew best. He was a doctor, after all.

Dr Nagel was also kind. He never turned down anyone looking for help. He hadn't charged for his services in years. But if Peter ever wanted to be cuddled by that huge, stiff figure, his grandfather would surely not have managed such a gesture. When forced to say something tender, Dr Nagel would remark in an offhand way, 'I'm fond of you, you know.' And that was it.

• • •

Peter celebrated Christmas Eve 1938 with his grandfather and Fräulein Strecker. The cook had prepared a goose; the butler had set up a Christmas tree in the living room, and the maids had set the table with candles. They sang Hungarian and German Christmas carols while standing around the tree, and then Fräulein Strecker gave Peter a shawl she had knitted during the evenings, when she had lots of time to spare, and she gave Dr Nagel a scarf that she had also knitted. Dr Nagel gave Fräulein Strecker an envelope with money in it, which he advised her to spend on something pretty, and he gave Peter another envelope with money in it, which he advised him to save. Later, Fräulein Strecker gave Peter a kiss, the invisible traces of which took him several minutes to wipe away when she wasn't looking. And Dr Nagel patted Peter on the head twice. One of Dr Nagel's grateful patients had presented the old man with a blue parakeet named Bobbi who could say, 'Bobbi', and, 'Alleluia', and the bird was lavished with attention.

After Christmas, winter dragged on without Dr Nagel ever mentioning that Peter might see his father. Then it was spring. Bobbi was tame, so tame that he didn't need a cage; all he had was a perch in the library. He flew around the room at his leisure, or sat on his perch babbling alleluias. One day the bird cleared its throat, 'ahem,' just the way Dr Nagel sometimes did, and then Dr Nagel began taking a greater interest in the bird. Soon he had taught him to say, 'How do you do?', and, 'Pleased to meet you.' The parakeet was not as shy as Peter. He enjoyed the doctor's company, often settling on the edge of his book while he was reading, and nibbling at the pages. For some reason, Dr

Nagel did not mind this damage to his library. One could tell which books he had been reading because the upper rims of the pages were jagged.

When Dr Nagel did not object, Bobbi began alighting on the rim of his tea glass in the afternoons, roosting there, rising upwards with the glass to the level of Dr Nagel's face when the doctor took a sip. It was Bobbi's custom to wait till the tea had cooled down before rather gingerly assuming his perch on the glass. But one day he was too eager and misjudged the rim: he landed too fast, tipping forwards and falling in headfirst.

Dr Nagel regarded the submerged victim. Only the very tip of Bobbi's tail feathers stuck out of the tea. Finally he pinched them between thumb and forefinger and hauled the bird out. Bobbi shook himself, scattering tea everywhere, and flew away. The old man looked after him coolly. 'Bobbi is too ambitious. But it is a doctor's responsibility to save lives,' he said, 'and saving lives is his pleasure.' He glanced at his grandson, his face solemn. Peter was glad that he had repressed a laugh.

By then it was summer. Germany, the maid and cook gossiped, was preparing for war. But the arrangements in Dr Nagel's house made politics seem peripheral. Breakfast, lunch, tea and dinner, those were the laws. And the boundaries that mattered were drawn in the house. Peter never entered the formal living room without being invited, nor the library, until he was called for afternoon tea. His grandfather's study was no more than a dark, closed door to him, the room behind off limits. Dr Nagel had never once invited his grandson inside. He occasionally summoned him into his dressing room, just for a minute, to see a family heirloom stored in one of the huge wardrobes. Even the ground outside was divided into territory that he could visit – the lawn, where he played football by himself (the butler was too old and stiff to join him), the garden where he sat on summer days, or the little woods at the back that he could explore – and an out-of-bounds area – the fruit trees and the vegetable patch.

Peter might have been very lonely if his father had not stuck to his word and written to him faithfully in his ghastly scrawl. On every Saturday, without a single exception, a letter came from Laszlo Nagel to his most beloved son. And every Saturday in the library, Peter's grandfather reluctantly read the letter aloud, leaving off the end, because it was too personal, too hot-hearted, such an embarrassment; as if the contents of the letter hadn't been bad enough! Laszlo wrote to his son about such remarkable things: he sometimes devoted an entire letter to a film he had seen, describing it with such detail that Peter could see it for himself, lying on his bed, looking at his window. Or Laszlo wrote about Thea, that she had a suitor, a nice young man who wanted to marry her. That her cooking had got much better since then, because she was practising for her future husband. And her mood was as even-tempered as one could wish. Frau Bilka also earned a letter now and again. The pigeons were on the rampage since Herr Bauer had 'left', and she was at her wits' end. 'More next week!' he always wrote, before signing off with many endearments to his son.

'Laszlo is too passionate about things,' Dr Nagel complained, handing the letter to Peter. 'The rest you can read yourself.'

It was autumn again. A year had passed. 'Fifty-two letters I've read to you,' groaned Dr Nagel, opening Peter's letter on a Saturday afternoon. 'And he is just a stranger to me.' He frowned, looking at the first lines, and muttered 'Dearest most beloved son,' his frown ploughing long furrows across his face. 'This time it's about another film he's seen.'

'Ahem. I begin …' he said, and began. He read in a quiet, neutral tone until he reached, 'More next week.' And abruptly he was finished, handing the letter to Peter, with a last editorial sigh.

'Your father is full of fiery feeling. It has always been like that, so you are lucky to be in my care,' he added.

For Christmas 1939, they ate goose again, and Fräulein Strecker gave them each hand-embroidered handkerchiefs. Germany had gone to war, won that war and expanded its borders, and was now rumbling noisily. 'Countries can rumble,' wrote Peter's father, 'before they explode. But here in the middle of the explosion, life is safe, life is comfortable. Yesterday I took Thea to the cinema. Her husband, the soldier, has been stationed in Poland, and she misses him. I assured her that life is not the same for me without her cooking. I did not tell her that I'm perfectly content eating sausages and liquorice every single evening.' Spring, summer, autumn. 'One hundred and four letters,' said Peter miserably.

Germany had gone to war again. For

Christmas 1940, Fräulein Strecker gave them hand-sewn wallets.

'Ahem,' said Dr Nagel, and unfolded the 117th letter from his son Laszlo Nagel to his grandson Peter Nagel. How many more letters could there be, wondered the boy, before they were no longer necessary because he would see his father again.

'City life,' wrote Peter's father, 'is neither boring nor dangerous for a good-luck man. Sit back in your chair and listen to the adventures I had this week at three different parties.'

'And how is Bobbi?' he wrote another time. 'Perhaps you can teach him to say something useful like, 'Help! Help!' Dr Nagel grimaced reading this aloud.

His grandfather had allowed him to take his father's photograph from the living room. Now it stood on Peter's desk, and he could look into his faher's dark eyes while he wrote, 'Dear Papa, You mustn't make suggestions concerning Bobbi.' If only he could read his father's letters himself. 'Perhaps you can write a little more neatly.'

'I will try to write neatly,' Peter's father wrote back in an entirely legible first sentence. But then his enthusiasm for what he had to say took over and his words spilled in a torrential jumble down the page.

Spring. Summer. Autumn. One hundred and fifty-six letters. For Christmas 1941, Fräulein Strecker gave them framed pictures she had painted herself. Dr Nagel's picture showed a majestic blue parakeet in full flight, his wingspan as enormous as an eagle's. For Peter, she had chosen one of the historical subjects they had covered in that year's lessons: her painting featured a pyramid, a camel with red fur standing in profile at the base of the building. The boy felt related to the camel, somehow. He managed to go for one entire week at a time without hearing from his father. Fräulein Strecker's parakeet was said to be hanging in Dr Nagel's study, while the pyramid and camel were propped on Peter's dresser.

Two hundred and eight letters. 'I have been seeing quite a bit of Thea these days,' wrote Laszlo Nagel to his son. 'I took her dancing to console her. It is a tragedy what happened to her husband, but it is a common enough tragedy these days. Her baby is due next month, but she danced up a storm.'

Soon after that Christmas, on a Saturday, a miracle happened. A letter from Peter's father arrived. From his vantage point on the wall, Peter could see that there was something different about it. He tried to get a better look at the envelope as the postman handed it to the butler, but the postman was in a hurry, and inconsiderately block his view. Time seemed frozen that morning unable to move forward to lunch and the visit afterwards in the library. At last, the week's best moment arrived. The envelope was indeed different. And the letter inside was different too. It was typed, so that Peter could understand every word, and he did not once need to ask his grandfather for assistance.

You haven't been the only one to suffer at the hands of my handwriting,' his father wrote, explaining that a close friend had given him a typewriter for Christmas, although it was hard to find typewriters now, even in Berlin, because of the War. 'This real office machinery is just another piece of luck,' wrote Laszlo Nagel to his son, and signed off with a hundred fatherly kisses that did not embarrass him, because they were typed, and his grandfather did not have to see them.

From that day on, his father's letters were his, and his alone.

'Never be concerned about me,' wrote his father. 'Despite the war, I am having a very good time. Despite your absence, which I regret so very much, every day, at least once an hour, my most beloved son.'

It seemed that all anyone did in Berlin these days was celebrate. There were big parties every evening. Frau Bilka and Dr Schneider took turns inviting the residents of the house for tea.

'Last night I took Thea, to a ballroom dance. She was the hit of the evening. She wore a huge red frock with a stiff petticoat underneath. She asked after you, of course, as she always does.'

Peter wrote back about the bicycle he had found in a field, just abandoned in a field, which no owner had come to claim. In truth, Peter didn't have a bicycle because he had never found one and his grandfather felt they were too dangerous for such a young boy. 'My bicycle is bright red with the loudest horn you can imagine. I ride very well now, very fast, especially downhill.'

'And I,' wrote Peter's father, 'have bought myself a motor cycle. It is black, with a side-car in which I sometimes take friends for a drive. Frau Bilka has been begging me for a ride.'

Fifty typed letters came, and then it was Christmas again.

• • •

One late summer afternoon in 1943, when Peter was already eleven years old, the house felt different. He had eaten breakfast with his grandfather as usual, and had his lessons with Fräulein Strecker until lunchtime, as usual. Lunch had proceeded normally. Afterwards, he had seen Fräulein Strecker out the door, and gone to his room to study. He was now judged old enough not to need an afternoon nap, and since it was no longer required, he had discovered the sweetness of sleeping in the afternoon. That day he began a new letter to his father, writing to him about a wild dog he had met while riding his bicycle. The dog had jumped up at him, frothing at the mouth, and nearly toppled him from his bike, but he had pumped his legs so quickly that he had managed to escape. Several sentences into this account of his outstanding courage, Peter grew aware of his bed, and the comforts it offered if he stretched out and closed his eyes a little. His head deep in the pillow, he heard a muffled rumble outside the house. He sat up. A car was leaving the driveway. Peter did not ask himself who was in it. He was too sleepy to care.

Later, when he went downstairs, he noticed at once that something had changed about the house. It was immersed in silence, but then it always was. Yet this silence felt different.

A year had passed since Bobbi the parakeet had suddenly said, 'Dammit.' The curse had shaken up the little family of master and servants. Dr Nagel did not know which of the staff was using bad language in front of the parakeet, or perhaps even worse, trying deliberately to teach such language to the bird, contaminating its vocabulary. Peter's grandfather hated feeling suspicious and solved the mystery by giving Bobbi to the town priest, who soon straightened his language out again. So Bobbi was gone, and no other foreign sound had replaced his chirping. Nevertheless, the silence in Dr Nagel's house had a certain tone, that was different on this particular afternoon.

After some time, Peter heard running water in the kitchen. He found the cook at her business. 'Your grandfather,' she said, 'has gone to visit a friend in Budapest. He will be back by nightfall.'

Without any danger of running into his grandfather, Peter Nagel wandered around the house. Without any plan in mind, he drifted inexorably towards the area where he was not allowed. He felt himself swept on a current of curiosity towards his grandfather's study.

The heavy brass door handle was high up on the door, at Peter's shoulder level. He looked at it with admiration. That golden handle was familiar to his grandfather's palm, the old man held it several times a day. An unimaginable period of time lay between Peter's eleven years and the age required to be allowed to touch that handle. He brushed it with his fingertips and jumped back with respect. It was cold to the touch. As he studied it, he saw that it could have another function. One could hang on to it. One could hang on to it, with all of one's weight, and it was sure not to budge. It must be a wonderful feeling, to hang from that door handle, thought Peter. Since the door was bound to be locked, there could be no harm in trying.

He placed both hands firmly around the handle, and slowly took his feet from the ground. The handle went down. The door swung open.

From the doorway he saw a wide dark desk at a window that overlooked the back garden. Bookshelves towered along the opposite wall. One shelf was lined with big bottles. Inside the bottle he could see floating objects that looked like dolls. Bottled dolls. How peculiar.

Peter took one step inside, and when this did not cause him to be struck at once by a bolt of lightning, he took another step. Fräulein Strecker's painting of a parakeet hung right near the door. He took another step. And then another. The bottles contained very tiny naked babies.

On another shelf stood more bottles, these with odd pieces of flesh that looked like ordinary but ancient butcher's meat. The smell was ugly, sour. The other shelves were full of dark, heavy books that looked like bibles but when he pulled several out and opened them, they proved to have gruesome illustrations of various kinds of disease and diseased people. Peter stopped every so often and trained his ears towards the door. The grasshoppers droned in the back garden.

Presumably he would hear the car returning. He relaxed and resumed his investigation. Against another wall was a chest with dozens of drawers, each holding tablets of different colours and sizes. On the desk there was a glass half full of gold liquid next to the typewriter. He sniffed at the glass: alcohol. He pulled open a desk drawer. Pens, pencils, desk supplies. He pulled open another drawer. Paper, in all different sizes and colours. He slid open yet another drawer and found a plain box.

He stopped to listen for a car. Nothing. Then he pulled the box out, opened it. It was nearly bursting with folded pages. Letters. He removed the top one and was confused. He recognised his own handwriting. They were letters he had written to his father. He pawed through them, forgetting their order, mixing them up. He glanced at them, each word a slash of embarrassment. What rubbish he had written. And his grandfather had read it all! All of his made up anecdotes, his false cheer, his boasting. His red bicycle. Peter replaced the letters, and looked back into the drawer. There was another box, and inside that another collection of his letters to his father. Now something was dawning on him.

He looked back at the typewriter. A piece of paper was wound around the roll, and had several lines typed on it. It was a letter that began, 'Dearest Most Beloved Son.'

• • •

Peter went on writing to his father in the same cheerful tone. He made a fool of himself knowingly now. He elaborated about the bicycle. And he read every line of his father's replies, trying to feel the same delight at the cheery news, at the affection he had never had from his grandfather. What else could he do? He could not admit to Dr Nagel that he had snooped in his study. And he did not have courage to ask for the truth.

The situation was changing anyway. Anxiety hung in the air. On the street people said the Germans were coming. Soon the cook said it openly in the kitchen at home. When Dr Nagel heard the servants speaking about the Germans, he was angry. He went into the kitchen and he said, 'Time will heal all. Stop worrying about the Nazis. The Germans are not coming. I know what I am talking about.' Since he had always and invariably known what he was talking about, the staff felt ashamed. For a while, they believed him.

Then the whispering began again. The

Germans are coming. Peter's father is in big trouble; Peter's father conspired. Peter's father was caught.

This time, Dr Nagel confronted them individually. He went into the kitchen to see the cook, he went to the cellar to see the maid who was cleaning there, to the garage to see the butler who was polishing the car there, to the garden to see the gardener. 'Listen,' he demanded 'Stop this foolish chatter. I'm an old man and I can't stand it. As a doctor, I understand something of the ways of the world, do I not?'

They agreed, that he did.

'And so you can believe me when I tell you, as a doctor: the Germans are not coming.'

And again, they relaxed, they believed him. He was the town doctor. It was Christmas, anyway. Fräulein Strecker had made paper flowers. At the end of February, the rumours began again. The town was just five kilometres from the new German border.

Their town would be the first to go. The Germans are coming; Peter's father conspired; he made false passports for Jews; he's been executed. Peter's father is dead.

On the second of March 1944, Dr Nagel went to the bank. When he returned, he had lunch as usual. After lunch, he had the staff assemble around his dining table. He invited the neighbours as well. He poured everyone a sherry. The table was crowded, the way it had been on the day of Laszlo's wedding to Dalia. 'The Germans are not coming,' he said. 'I know. And in order to prove it, I am going to pay out six months of wages ahead of time. Would I do that if the Germans were coming?'

And solemnly, the way he did everything, he passed out envelopes. Inside each envelope was a large wad of money, exactly the sum that he owed for six months of work. After he had extracted a promise from each in turn that he could now have six months respite from their goose-like fear, he retired to his study, as he always did after lunch.

The butler had prepared a little speech of thanks that he was going to deliver at teatime that afternoon. The table was set in the library. But Dr Nagel did not arrive on time. After half an hour had passed, the tea was cold. The butler called Peter and said, 'Go knock on your grandfather's door, and remind him that it's tea time.'

Peter knocked. His guilty concience scolded him every time he passed the study. When his grandfather did not respond, he fetched the butler, and the butler knocked, and when there was no response, he fetched the cook, and she knocked.

The cook went in. She found Dr Nagel slumped at his desk, his arms dangling. His head on the typewriter covered the page had had been writing.

Peering in from the threshold, Peter watched the cook's hand travel to the old man's shoulder and then yank away, her head tip back slowly, her mouth inch open, her

eyes begin to bulge. A strange wobbling up her neck evidently carried the scream that at last tore the interminable quiet of the doctor's home.

When the undertaker came for Dr Nagel he glanced at the last words of the deceased on the typewriter, and wondered a little.

Dearest Most Beloved Son,
Spring has finally made it to the north

'Bad luck,' the undertaker grumbled, as he always did. His profession had not inured him to a feeling of outrage about death. Perhaps it really was good luck. The next day, the Germans came.

• • •

A wise old woman, an optimist, who had lived a long time and seen all the patterns of life, once said: great unhappiness is always sandwiched between two seasons of great happiness. She made no specifications about the length of each season. What happened after the correspondence between Peter and his father came to an end still belongs to a season of unhappiness but it has a very happy ending, and the ending is worth mentioning. The old woman who knew about the inevitability of happiness was Peter's great-aunt. She lived in Budapest, and as Peter's last remaining relation, she took charge of him after his grandfather died.

Aunt Eva was so old that she herself had lost track of her age. Nevertheless, she was agile and cared a great deal about certain things. For instance, she cared about clothes. She had the largest wardrobe in all of Budapest, no closet could contain it. She kept her clothes in the master bedroom of her apartment – the hats and wigs covered the bed, and the dresses were hung like valuable paintings along the walls – and she slept in the maid's room. When Peter arrived, and she had recovered from an attack of delight and envy about the colour of his hair, she gave him the maid's bed, and uncomplainingly slept on the living room sofa. 'I'm asleep, so I don't notice the surroundings.'

He remained with Aunt Eva for more than a year, going through thick and thin with her in Budapest – but that is another story. Shortly after the war was finally over, but the misery in many parts of Europe had in no way abated, Aunt Eva and her nephew received a visitor from Germany. The visitor was terribly thin and very tired. She had travelled for days to reach Budapest, and she had a small child on her arm. It was Thea and her daughter.

It turned out that Peter's father had made up the story about Thea marrying a soldier. She had actually married Laszlo Nagel and they had had a child, named Hannah. So Peter had a small sister. And now he also had a mother.

Peter said goodbye to Aunt Eva, promising to visit her soon. Thea took him and Hannah back to the farm in southern Germany where she herself had grown up,